Conservation and Ecology of Marine Forage Fishes— Proceedings of a Research Symposium, September 2012

Edited by
Theresa Liedtke, U.S. Geological Survey;
Caroline Gibson, Northwest Straits Commission;
Dayv Lowry, Washington State Department of Fish and Wildlife; and
Duane Fagergren, Puget Sound Partnership

Open-File Report 2013–1035

U.S. Department of the Interior
U.S. Geological Survey

U.S. Department of the Interior
KEN SALAZAR, Secretary

U.S. Geological Survey
Marcia K. McNutt, Director

U.S. Geological Survey, Reston, Virginia: 2013

For more information on the USGS—the Federal source for science about the Earth, its natural and living resources, natural hazards, and the environment—visit *http://www.usgs.gov* or call 1–888–ASK–USGS

For an overview of USGS information products, including maps, imagery, and publications, visit *http://www.usgs.gov/pubprod*

To order this and other USGS information products, visit *http://store.usgs.gov*

Suggested citation:
Liedtke, Theresa, Gibson, Caroline, Lowry, Dayv, and Fagergren, Duane, eds., 2013, Conservation and Ecology of Marine Forage Fishes—Proceedings of a Research Symposium, September 2012: U.S. Geological Survey Open-File Report 2013-1035, 24 p.

Acknowledgments

The symposium organizing committee wishes to thank the many science and policy experts who contributed to the success of the symposium through presentation of their work, ideas, and thoughtful participation in discussions. This event would not have been possible without the leadership and support of the Northwest Straits Commission and sponsoring agencies.

We thank Adam Summers, Laurie Spaulding, and Kristy Kull at the University of Washington Friday Harbor Laboratories for the great facility, food, and on-site logistics; as well as Andrea Hood (Northwest Straits Commission) and Shannon Davis (FRIENDS of the San Juans) for taking detailed notes that were the basis for this document.

Special thanks to Brie Van Cleve (FB Van Cleve & Associates) for outstanding facilitation and support throughout the symposium, and to Joseph Gaydos (SeaDoc Society) and Kit Rawson (Tulalip Tribes) for skillfully facilitating the science and policy work groups.

Although this event was co-sponsored by the U.S. Geological Survey, comments and written reports made by speakers not affiliated with the USGS do not represent the views or position of the USGS.

NORTHWEST STRAITS
marine conservation initiative

Contents

Conservation and Ecology of Marine Forage Fishes—Proceedings of a Research Symposium, September 2012

Edited by
Theresa Liedtke, U.S. Geological Survey;
Caroline Gibson, Northwest Straits Commission;
Dayv Lowry, Washington State Department of Fish and Wildlife; and
Duane Fagergren, Puget Sound Partnership

Introduction and Background

Locally and globally, there is growing recognition of the critical roles that herring, smelt, sand lance, eulachon, and other forage fishes play in marine ecosystems. Scientific and resource management entities throughout the Salish Sea, agree that extensive information gaps exist, both in basic biological knowledge and parameters critical to fishery management. Communication and collaboration among researchers also is inadequate.

Building on the interest and enthusiasm generated by recent forage fish workshops and symposia around the region, the *2012 Research Symposium on the Conservation and Ecology of Marine Forage Fishes* was designed to elucidate practical recommendations for science and policy needs and actions, and spur further collaboration in support for the precautionary management of forage fish. This dynamic and productive event was a joint venture of the Northwest Straits Commission Forage Fish Program, U.S. Geological Survey (USGS), Washington Department of Fish and Wildlife (WDFW), and The Puget Sound Partnership.

The symposium was held on September 12–14, 2012, at the University of Washington, Friday Harbor Laboratories campus. Sixty scientists, graduate students, and fisheries policy experts convened; showcasing ongoing research, conservation, and management efforts targeting forage fish from regional and national perspectives. The primary objectives of this event were to: (1) review current research and management related to marine forage fish species; and (2) identify priority science and policy needs and actions for Washington, British Columbia, and the entire West Coast. Given the diversity of knowledge, interests, and disciplines surrounding forage fish on both sides of the international border, the organizing committee made a concerted effort to contact many additional experts who, although unable to attend, provided valuable insights and ideas to the symposium structure and discussions.

The value of the symposium format was highlighted in the closing remarks delivered by Joseph Gaydos, SeaDoc Society and Chair of the Puget Sound Science Panel. Dr. Gaydos' presentation referenced the 2011 paper by Murray Rudd in the journal *Conservation Biology,* "How research-prioritization exercises affect conservation policy." The paper points out that policy makers and funding agencies are more likely to gain a full understanding of issues when they are presented with research findings from an aligned research program. That is, compared to unaligned research strategies, where work is not based on identified research priorities.

Symposium Agenda

The gathering launched with a dinner of local wild salmon and provided networking opportunities for invited speakers and participants, many of whom traveled considerable distances, and had not previously met each other or had not previously visited Friday Harbor Laboratories. The symposium began with 1 full day of invited science and policy presentations, with a keynote address by Tim Essington;(University of Washington) designed to inform in-depth discussions on the second day. A brief questionnaire was circulated on day 1 to help elucidate recommendations for science and policy needs and actions to be discussed on day 2.

Day 2 included two facilitated working groups, with subsequent review in plenary session of the identified priority science and policy needs and actions for Washington, British Columbia, and the West Coast. The agenda was crafted to address the research and management review on day 1 and to engage the participants in discussion of the priority science and policy needs and actions on day 2. A poster session was held at the end of day 1 to supplement oral presentations, and to foster additional information exchange in preparation for the discussions on day 2. The complete list of symposium participants is presented in appendix A.

Day 1: Thursday September 13

- **Welcome and introductions:** Adam Summers, University of Washington/Friday Harbor Laboratories; Caroline Gibson, Northwest Straits Commission
- **Symposium goals:** Brie Van Cleve, facilitator (FB Van Cleve & Associates)
- **Forage fish management in Washington:** Dayv Lowry, Washington Department of Fish and Wildlife
- **Forage fish management in British Columbia:** Jennifer Boldt, Fisheries and Oceans Canada
- **Herring and the ecological effects of infectious and parasitic diseases:** Paul Hershberger, U.S. Geological Survey
- **Toxic contaminants and effects on adult herring and eggs:** James West, Washington Department of Fish and Wildlife
- **Landscape and seasonal patterns of fishes and jellyfish in Puget Sound surface waters:** Casey Rice, NOAA/ Northwest Fisheries Science Center
- **Temporal variation of pelagic forage fish around San Juan Island:** Emily Runnells, University of Washington
- **Seabird diets in the Salish Sea:** Scott Pearson, Washington Department of Fish and Wildlife

- *KEYNOTE*: **Advancing recommendations from the Lenfest Forage Fish Task Force:** Tim Essington, University of Washington

- **An iconoclastic view of herring and forage fish in the Salish Sea—match and mismatch between concern and ecology:** Douglas Hay, Nearshore Research
- **Native fish communities and habitat coupling: delivery of a nearshore energy subsidy by an offshore planktivore:** Jason Stockwell, University of Vermont
- **Regional marine food webs and modeling of energy flow:** Issac Kaplan, NOAA /Northwest Fisheries Science Center
- **Pacific sand lance burrowing/physiology:** Adam Summers, University of Washington/Friday Harbor Laboratories

- **Predator-prey interactions and status of forage species in the California current:** Julie Thayer, Farrallon Institute for Advanced Ecosystem Research
- **Forage fishes and adaptive ecosystem-based management planning:** Olav Ormseth, NOAA/ Alaska Fisheries Science Center
- **Analyzing management strategies for marine forage fishes:** Felipe Hurtado, University of Washington
- **Federal–state policies and the Coastal Pelagic Species Fisheries Management Plan:** Lorna Wargo, Washington Department of Fish and Wildlife
- **The Pacific Forage Fish Campaign-Strengthening U.S. Federal policy:** Steve Marx, Pew Environment Group
- **Poster session**

Day 2: Friday September 14

- **Key outcomes from day 1 and objectives for day 2:** Brie Van Cleve (FB Van Cleve & Associates)
- **Forage fish in Puget Sound: an anecdotal perspective:** Duane Fagergren, Puget Sound Partnership and Northwest Straits Commission
- **Puget Sound marine food web and forage fish monitoring workgroup:** Ken Dzinbal, Puget Sound Partnership
- **Framework for research and policy needs discussions:** Brie Van Cleve (FB Van Cleve & Associates)
- **Discussion groups:**
    - Science Needs: facilitated by Joseph Gaydos, SeaDoc Society
    - Policy Needs: facilitated by Kit Rawson, Tulalip Tribes
- **Summary of discussion groups, group consensus, and wrap up:** Brie Van Cleve (FB Van Cleve & Associates)

Symposium Presentations

Each invited speaker on day 1 provided a presentation abstract, included here in chronological order of delivery. In addition, several participants presented posters and the abstracts for those are presented in alphabetical order, based on the first author.

Presentation Abstracts

Forage Fish Management in Washington

Dayv Lowry, Washington Department of Fish and Wildlife

Forage fish are small, schooling fish that serve an integral role in marine food webs as consumers of plankton and primary consumers, and prey for other fish, birds, and marine mammals. Forage fish species in Washington include Pacific herring, various smelt, Pacific sand lance, northern anchovy, and Pacific sardine.

Though exploitation of forage fishes for human consumption in Washington has occurred for centuries, modern fisheries management began in earnest in 1971 with the establishment of the Puget Sound Baitfish Project. Since this time, the Department of Fish and Wildlife has, to varying degrees, studied the distribution, abundance, genetic variation, ecology, and fisheries exploitation of forage species, especially herring and surf smelt. In 1998, the Department developed a plan for the management of forage fish resources in Washington that was intended to guide resource management decisions, establish research and monitoring priorities, and shape fishing regulations in accordance with a precautionary approach to overall management. The plan was distinctive, at the time, in that it emphasized the ecological role of forage fishes and explicitly stated that harvest would be foregone as needed to ensure adequate forage fish were left to accomplish their ecological role.

Since the late 1990s, the Department has dedicated moderate resources to the research and management of forage fishes, though this trend has been changing since the mid-2000s. Commercial fisheries currently exist for herring, surf smelt, anchovy (largely inactive), and sardine (coastal waters outside 3 NM), and recreational fisheries exist for herring and surf smelt. Fisheries for eulachon, or Columbia River smelt, were progressively reduced, and ultimately closed entirely in 2010, in response to listing of this species as Threatened under the Endangered Species Act. With growing international recognition of the ecological importance of forage fish, and the consequences of their overexploitation, scrutiny of Washington's management has increased in recent years.

The Department is currently part of a coordinated regional effort to re-evaluate forage fish management practices and research priorities. This effort also includes Tribal co-managers, the Northwest Straits Commission, the SeaDoc Society, the federal government (USGS and NOAA Fisheries), academic partners (University of Washington, Western Washington University), the Department of Fisheries and Oceans Canada, and various community action and stakeholder groups. Leveraging this recent enthusiasm, numerous research projects have begun in Washington in the past few years that have the potential to guide forage fish management in the future.

Forage Fish Management in British Columbia, Canada

Jennifer Boldt[1], Tom Therriault[1], Jaclyn Cleary[1], Jake Schweigert[1], Linnea Flostrand[1], Douglas Hay[2], Lisa Mijacika[1]

[1]*Fisheries and Oceans Canada.*
[2]*Nearshore Research.*

Important forage fish species in British Columbia (BC), Canada include Pacific herring (*Clupea pallasi*), Pacific sardine (*Sardinops sagax*), eulachon (*Thaleichthys pacificus*), sand lance (*Ammodytes hexapterus Pallas*), surf smelt (*Hypomesus pretiosus*), and anchovies (*Engraulis mordax*). Many of these species have also comprised economically and/or socially (culturally) important fisheries in BC. Within BC waters some stocks of these species are non-migratory, some are migratory, and others migrate across international boundaries. Where fisheries management plans exist, Fisheries and Oceans Canada (DFO) applies a precautionary approach. In general, this approach is about being cautious when scientific knowledge is uncertain, and not using the absence of adequate scientific information as a reason to postpone or fail to take action to avoid serious harm to fish stocks or their ecosystem. This widely accepted approach is an essential part of sustainable fisheries management. In addition to policies on incorporating the Precautionary Approach, the new national Sustainable Fisheries Framework in Canada contains policies for adopting an ecosystem based approach to fisheries management including: Managing Impacts of Fishing on Benthic Habitat, Communities and Species, and a policy on New Fisheries for Forage Species.

Herring and the Ecological Effects of Infectious and Parasitic Diseases

Paul Hershberger, U.S. Geological Survey

For unconfirmed reasons, forage fish populations periodically undergo large oscillations in population size and species assemblage shifts. These well-documented changes often resonate throughout multiple trophic levels; as such, an understanding of proximate and ultimate causes of forage fish population change is necessary to successfully manage codependent marine resources, including Pacific salmonids and marine mammals. Here, I present lines of evidence supporting the hypothesis that Pacific herring populations throughout the NE Pacific are impacted by diseases caused by endemic pathogens, including viral hemorrhagic septicemia virus (VHSV), erythrocytic necrosis virus (ENV) and Ichthyophonus. Examples include the decline and failed recovery of herring populations in Prince William Sound, Alaska, and the recent shifts in age structure among herring populations in Puget Sound, Washington. Ultimate drivers of these proximate disease impacts are being addressed using a well-controlled reductionistic approach, and predictive tools are being developed that will be capable of forecasting the potential for future disease impacts to herring populations.

Toxic Contaminants and Effects on Adult Herring and Eggs

James E. West, Washington Department of Fish and Wildlife
Sandra M. O'Neill, NOAA/Northwest Fisheries Science Center

Pacific herring are exposed to a wide range of toxic contaminants in Puget Sound, at levels that may affect their health and reproductive success, as well as pose a risk to the health of humans who consume them. Herring and other small, schooling, pelagic planktivorous fishes also play an important role in the trophic transfer of bioaccumulative toxic contaminants in Puget Sound, resulting in exposure to predators higher in the food chain (e.g., Pacific salmon, rockfishes, lingcod, piscivorous seabirds, and marine mammals). The nearshore benthic spawning behavior of Pacific herring also places their eggs and embryos at risk of exposure to contaminants, because input of many toxic contaminants in Puget Sound occurs at the land-sea interface. In this talk we review results from a long-term monitoring study of toxic contaminants in adult herring, and focus on spatial and temporal trends for three major contaminant groups—(1) polychlorinated biphenyls, or PCBs; (2) brominated flame retardants (or PBDEs); and (3) hydrocarbons, resulting from oil spills and burning fossil fuels (polycyclic aromatic hydrocarbons, or PAHs). We discuss the health risks to this species from exposure to these contaminants, and a frame of reference for the safety of this species as seafood for humans. We also present results of a one-time survey on exposure of spawned herring embryos to environmental PAHs, representing five major spawning stocks in Puget Sound and the Southern Strait of Georgia.

Landscape and Seasonal Patterns of Fishes and Jellyfish in Puget Sound Surface Waters—Preliminary Results

Casey Rice[1], Correigh Greene[1], Linda Rhodes[1], Brian Beckman[1], Jeff Cordell[2], Anne Baxter[1], Jason Hall[1], Josh Chamberlin[1], Hans Daubenberger[3], Hiroo Imaki[1], Scott Stelzner[3], Kurt Fresh[1]

[1]*NOAA/Northwest Fisheries Science Center,*
[2]*University of Washingto.*
[3]*Port Gamble/S'Kallam Tribe.*
[4]*Squaxin Tribe*

Recent declines in pelagic fish species such as herring and alterations in coastal foodwebs have raised the question of how people affect the pelagic ecosystem. We are examining how natural habitat features and human alterations to shoreline habitats and their local catchments may influence patterns in species abundance and composition from lower to middle trophic levels by integrating landscape analysis into a broad surface trawling design sampling over 80 sites monthly across Puget Sound in 2011.

Similar to data from 2003, we observed clear differences in the biomass composition among the subbasins of Puget Sound, with fish dominating in the northern areas, and jellyfish dominant in central, south, and Hood Canal. Strong spatial structure is also apparent in microbial activity and plankton community composition. Analysis to characterize spatial and temporal patterns in the biota and relate them to abiotic variables is ongoing.

Temporal Variation of Pelagic Forage Fish Around San Juan Island

Emily Runnells, University of Washington

I am testing the hypothesis that seabird feeding activity in Cattle Pass, San Juan Islands, Washington, has decreased in comparison to the mid-1990s, along with decreases in the abundance of small, pelagic fish. Data collection included land-based seabird surveys and multi-frequency acoustic surveys that were used to determine the distribution and abundance of forage fish. These seabird and forage fish surveys replicated the methods used by J. Zamon (unpublished) in the mid-1990s. To date, I have done a preliminary analysis of interdecadal variation. It appears that there is a significant decrease in seabird foraging activity between decades. The area integrated backscatter (a measure of forage fish abundance) shows a consistent trend between decades, throughout the summer season. There are yearly differences in both seabird foraging activity and forage fish abundance, showing similar variation, with some discrepancy. Analyzing the top 30m and top 10m of the water column separately, to test for changes in spatial distribution of forage fish, indicated that the upper water column was less variable between decades. These interesting patterns lead me to explain my next steps in analyzing the relationship between seabird foraging and forage fish abundance and distribution.

Seabird Diets in the Salish Sea and Northern California Current

Scott Pearson[1], Michael Schrimpf[2], Peter Hodum[3], Tom Good[4], Julia K. Parrish[2], Jane Dolliver[2]

[1]Washington Department of Fish and Wildlife.
[2]University of Washington.
[3]University of Puget Sound.
[4]NOAA/Northwest Fisheries Science Center

Seabird diet has been used as an indicator of fish populations, fishery recruitment, climate change and shorter-term climate events, and to understand food web relationships, especially in endangered ecosystems such as the Salish Sea. To identify information gaps and summarize what is known about seabird diet in the Salish Sea and northern California Current, we created a database of seabird literature that allows users to summarize data available for specific prey and predator taxa, time periods, and/or geographic regions. The database allows users to identify seabird-species specific diets and also identify the suite of seabird species that eat a given species of fish. For example, the studies in the database identify 12 seabird species consume Pacific herring (*Clupea harengus pallasi*). The distribution of diet studies was not uniform across time, with some seabird species having much more coverage than others. Several species of alcids had the longest continuous diet data, with periods of study extending 10 or more years in the late 1990s and early 2000s.

An alternative way to assess changes in seabird diet is to compare results from contemporary and historic studies. Our contemporary research on rhinoceros auklet (*Cerorhinca monocerata*) diet coupled with work conducted in the 1970s is an example from the database of how seabird diet can be used to assess ecosystem changes over time. In this study, we sampled auklet diet in the Salish Sea (Protection Island), on the outer coast of Washington (Destruction Island), and at the confluence of both environments (Tatoosh Island). Over 5,729 fish samples (968 bill loads) were collected from auklets during three sampling trips per island per season (2006-2010). In the Salish Sea, Pacific sandlance (*Ammodytes hexapterus*) and to a lesser degree herring made up the majority of the diet, while the diet on the coast was more diverse. Despite differences in size of fish among islands, the average weight and energy (KJ/g) per bill load did not differ between the Salish Sea and the coast because birds compensated by returning with more fish per bill load.

When we put our results in an historic context, average bill load weight and diet composition has not changed between the 1970s and today in the Salish Sea. Our work addresses the need for seabird diet data on a particular species in specific regions, while also identifying which regions and species may require more attention in the future.

KEYNOTE: Challenges and Opportunities in the Conservation and Management of Forage Fishes: Advancing Recommendations from the Lenfest Forage Fish Task Force

Tim Essington, University of Washington

Small, schooling pelagic species often play critical roles in food webs as conduits of energy from lower trophic level species to upper trophic level species (e.g., salmon, rockfish, marine mammals, sea birds).

Managing fisheries that target these species—often for bait or reduction to fishmeal and fish oil—is made problematic by highly variable population dynamics and by the fact that these species are often easy to target and catch in large numbers even when population densities are low. Managing fisheries to protect their vital ecosystem services requires attention to localized depletion, identifying and protecting foraging opportunities for dependent predators, and developing robust indicators that can warn of ecological effects. The Lenfest Forage Fish Task Force recently completed its final report and recommendations regarding the management of forage fish fisheries that account for their unique life histories and ecological roles. One key recommendation was an operational precautionary approach that defined levels of knowledge about stock health and ecosystem effects and appropriate limit and target reference points that should apply for each level. Here I review those recommendations, comment on their application to U.S. and Canadian fisheries, and also review the options for economic valuation of forage species that account for their benefits to fisheries and non-market species.

An Iconoclastic View of Herring and Forage Fish in the Salish Sea—Match and Mismatch between Concern and Ecology

Doulas Hay, Nearshore Research

In general, concerns about forage fish species (FFS) in the Salish Sea (SS) are related to decreases in abundance or diminishing spatial distribution. More specific concerns are related to changes in age composition, especially recent reductions in the frequency of older, larger fish and changes in spawning time. Organizations, mainly NGOs, advocating progressive changes in policy in the marine environment have focused on curtailing fisheries as a solution to the apparent problems. Such action often may be warranted but not necessarily for all regions or all FFS in the SS. Further, the focus on fisheries has deflected attention away from habitat issues that jeopardize health and habitats used by FFS. Important FFS habitats may be at risk from industrial developments and mariculture in important herring spawning areas. The focus on fisheries as a problem can also undermine the general appreciation of climate change impacts on the biology and ecology of FFS in the SS.

Of all FFS in the SS we know most about herring. Herring spawn in shallow, coastal areas. Records of spawning locations, collected since the 1920s, indicate that repeated use of specific spawning locations varies. Some spawning locations are abandoned but a review of the distribution of roe-herring fishing areas shows no evidence of cessation (or serial depletion) of spawning attributable to fishing. However even simple overviews of the distribution of coastline industrialization show substantial activity in important spawning areas and the long-term consequences are uncertain. Protecting herring spawning habitat can be difficult for management agencies because spawning locations vary in time. Also, there is increasing evidence that spawning locations can vary annually as a function of temperature and perhaps other oceanographic phenomena. Demographic changes occurring through the North Pacific also may be important because older, larger herring tend to spawn earlier and may use different locations than younger herring spawning later. Compounding this complexity is a striking decrease in size-at-age of herring—a phenomenon that may be climate-related and perhaps cyclical over long periods. Recent (2000-2012) size- at-age patterns resemble that of the early 1950s. There also is evidence of recent fundamental changes in maturation biology with relative ovary size increasing.

Native Fish Communities and Habitat Coupling: Delivery of a Nearshore Energy Subsidy by an Offshore Planktivore

Jason Stockwell, University of Vermont, Rubenstein Ecosystem Science Laboratory

In ecosystems where native fish species have been greatly reduced or extirpated, ecological processes such as transport of energy and nutrients across habitats or ecosystems may be lost to the detriment of remaining native species. We hypothesized that fall spawning migrations of rehabilitated Lake Superior cisco (*Coregonus artedi*) provide a spatial resource subsidy from the offshore pelagic to the nearshore benthic community over winter, in the form of energy-rich cisco eggs, when alternate prey production is likely low. We tested this hypothesis using fish population demographics, diet and stable isotope analyses, and bioenergetics modeling. Our results suggest that cisco eggs represent 16% of lake whitefish (*C. clupeaformis*) annual consumptive demand on a biomass basis, but 35% on an energetic basis because of their high energy density (> 10 kJ·g wet^{-1}). Stable isotope analyses corroborated these results, and suggest other nearshore fish species also may rely on cisco eggs. Cisco eggs likely play an important role for post-spawn recovery and future reproductive output of whitefish. In the other Great Lakes, where cisco populations remain very low, the offshore-to-inshore ecological link present in Lake Superior has been replaced by non-native planktivorous species which spawn in spring, have smaller eggs, and shorter incubation periods. Our work suggests rehabilitation of native fishes may provide additional benefits beyond simple predator-prey considerations.

Potential Impacts of Depleting Forage Species in the California Current

Isaac Kaplan, NOAA/Northwest Fisheries Science Center

Harvests of lower-trophic level species may be in direct competition with forage needs of other species. Colleagues and I have applied two ecosystem models of the California Current to test the impacts on other parts of the ecosystem of harvesting euphausiids, forage fish, mackerel, and mesopelagic fish such as myctophids. We estimated the abundance that would lead to maximum sustainable yield for these four groups individually, but found that depleting forage groups to these levels can have both positive and negative effects on other species. The most common impacts were on predators of forage groups, some of which showed declines of >20% when forage groups were depleted to 40% of unfished levels, a level commonly believed to be sustainable for single species. Depletion of euphausiids and forage fish had the largest impact on other species. Though higher trophic level species such as groundfish are often managed on the basis of reference points that can reduce biomass to below half of unfished levels, this level of forage species removal is likely to impact the abundance of other fishery target species and other groups in the food web. These results are consistent with a related global study (Smith et al. 2011 *Science* 333:1147–1150) that considered five ecosystems and three alternate ecosystem modeling frameworks.

Pacific sand Lance Burrowing/Morphology

Adam P. Summers[1], Jordan Balaban[2], Nicholas Gidmark[3], Joseph J. Bizzarro[1]

[1]University of Washington.Friday Harbor Laboratories
[2]University of Rhode Island.
[3]Brown University.

Sand lance are small forage fish that spend a substantial amount of time buried in the substrate. We have investigated their preference for certain grain sizes, the kinematics of burrowing, and the forces needed to penetrate the substrate. Using small (30-50) schools of sand lance in tanks with a single size class of sediment we determined they can burrow in everything from small gravel to mud. However, when presented with a choice between sediments of different sizes they preferred a coarse sand with grain size from 0.5-1 mm. The next size class larger was preferred over the next size class smaller and other size classes were barely tolerated if there was a choice. We used high speed video and x-ray videography to quantify the kinematics of burrowing. Sand lance usually contact the substrate at a steep angle and, holding their head still they drive the head and anterior third of their body into the substrate. Then the tail becomes motionless and the anterior of the body undulates to draw the rest of the fish under. Using a polymer molding compound we made epoxy replicas of the anterior third of several sand lance then clamped these models in a material testing system and drove them into packed and unpacked wet substrates. It requires significantly more force to penetrate packed substrates but preference experiments showed sand lance do not prefer the unpacked over the packed. We expect this is because they are making their substrate choice visually rather than by testing their burrowing ability.

Forage Fish Ecology and Management in the California Current with an Emphasis on Predator Needs

Julie Thayer, Farallon Institute for Advanced Ecosystem Research

Mid-trophic level forage species are an important component of marine food webs which directly support marine birds, mammals and fish of societal concern, but are generally under-studied in most marine ecosystems. In the California Current system (CCS), primary forage species include a variety of coastal pelagic fish (e.g., sardine, anchovy), juveniles of predatory fishes (e.g., age 0-1 rockfish, hake), and invertebrates (e.g., squid, krill). Forage species management within the CCS falls under various jurisdictions including federal and state agencies, and tribes. The California Marine Life Management Act (MLMA) and the federal Magnuson-Stevens Fisheries Conservation and Management and Sustainable Fisheries Acts require that ecological interactions and dependencies be incorporated into fishery management plans (FMPs) and regulatory decisions, but this has been infrequently implemented. U.S. management agencies are now grappling with development of ecosystem fisheries management plans (EFMP). I will provide an overview of forage fish ecology, importance and management in the CCS, with an emphasis on forage in relation to predator needs. The increased importance of forage species to commercial fisheries revenue and aquaculture increases the urgency of improving management and understanding the implications of removing forage species from the ecosystem.

Management and Monitoring of Forage Fishes in Alaska

Olav Ormseth and Stephani Zador, NOAA/Alaska Fisheries Science Center

In Alaska, the phrase "forage fishes" can mean several different things. As is the case elsewhere, forage fishes are generally small fishes that serve a critical ecosystem role as prey for larger fishes, seabirds, and marine mammals. But this group comprises many different species with a wide variety of biological characteristics, vulnerability to human impacts, and regulatory mechanisms. Forage fishes are often juvenile stages of species, such as walleye pollock, whose adult forms are the targets of major federal and state fisheries. Pacific herring is a key forage species that is targeted by commercial and subsistence fisheries in state waters. Federal management also recognizes a "forage fish" group of diverse taxa, from smelts to krill, for which all directed fishing is prohibited and retention and processing are strictly limited. Despite the variety of forage species, most of this group shares the central challenge of monitoring temporal and spatial trends in abundance. In Alaska, very little survey effort is directed towards forage fish assessment. We are currently exploring the use of different proxies for abundance including bycatch rates in hydroacoustic surveys, patterns of seabird productivity, trends in predator diet composition, and changes in mean size. We will present an overview of forage fishes and their management in Alaska, highlight research needs, and offer some suggestions for monitoring abundance.

Analyzing Management Strategies for Marine Forage Fishes

Felipe HurtadoFerro, University of Washington

Forage fish support some of the world's largest fisheries, comprising around 37% of global marine fish catches, and are key components of marine food webs, converting energy from lower trophic levels and supporting larger fish, seabirds and marine mammals. Despite their ecological and economic importance, forage fish are also highly variable, being influenced by environmental and oceanic conditions, resulting in massive and unpredictable fluctuations in abundance. These factors present managers with multiple and conflicting objectives, multiple stakeholders and high levels of uncertainty. The management strategy evaluation (MSE) framework was developed as a response to these challenges. MSE involves assessing the consequences and effects of a range of management strategies, explicitly considering uncertainty, and presenting results in a way that clearly shows the trade-offs in performance across a range of management objectives.

In this talk, I will present two examples of MSE for two contrasting sardine stocks: Pacific sardine and Japanese sardine. Pacific sardine is a healthy stock managed conservatively with relatively low exploitation rates, while the Japanese stock is currently at very low abundance levels and has been fished intensively. In both cases different management strategies are evaluated, with special attention given to strategies that incorporate environmental factors.

Federal-State Policies and the Coastal Pelagic Species Fisheries Management Plan

Lorna Wargo, Washington Department of Fish and Wildlife

Forage fish management along the Washington coast is guided by both federal and state policies and regulations. The Pacific Fishery Management Council (Council), one of eight regional fishery councils in the United States, is responsible for setting fishery management policy and developing management measures for a suite of forage fish species in the Exclusive Economic Zone (3-200 miles) off the coasts of Washington, Oregon, and California. The Washington Fish and Wildlife Commission establishes policies for fish resource utilization in state waters (0-3 miles); the Department of Fish and Wildlife is charged with implementing these policies through regulations. Two documents provide the framework for forage fish management in Washington: the Council's Coastal Pelagics Fishery Management Plan, and the Fish and Wildlife Commission's Forage Fish Management Plan, A plan for managing the forage fish resources and fisheries of Washington. Implementation of these comes with a host of challenges to understand the importance of forage fish in maintaining a healthy marine ecosystem, to set appropriate harvest levels and to address the potential for new fisheries to develop.

Pacific Forage Fish Campaign: Strengthening U.S. Federal Policy

Steve Marx, Pew Environment Group

The Pacific Fish Conservation Campaign is part of the Pew Environment Group's national Forage Fish Conservation Initiative. The Pacific Campaign works to suspend the expansion of fisheries on forage stocks unless and until an ecosystem-based approach can be implemented that conserves the prey base for all marine life. Currently, the campaign is working within the Pacific Fishery Management Council process to prevent new fisheries from developing on unmanaged or unfished forage species such as saury, sandlance and lanternfish, until adequate science and management measures are in place to ensure an ecologically sustainable fishery.

Under existing law and regulations, new fisheries on unmanaged forage species can develop in the absence of any science and/or regulation. The campaign is also working to ensure that the Pacific Council explicitly incorporates ecological considerations into the management of existing forage fisheries on species such as Pacific sardine, market squid, northern anchovy and mackerel. This means that fishery managers must identify the impacts of forage removals on the ecosystem and other fisheries, assess the dietary needs of predators in the ecosystem, and make sure that they are leaving enough in the water to account for those needs and to maintain the role that forage species serve as prey. While the campaign is currently engaged at the federal level, they are also working to enact similar precautionary forage policies in state waters. The ultimate goal of this campaign and Pew's other national efforts are to help implement an ecosystem-based approach to fisheries management; protecting forage species as the cornerstone of healthy and productive marine ecosystems is the first step.

Poster Abstracts

Juvenile Wild Chinook migrating and rearing in the San Juan Islands prefer herring but rely on sandlance

Russel Barsh, Gene Helfman, Donna Adams, Julia Loyd, Madrona Murphy, Dennis Rosenman, and C.J. Wilson
KWIAHT

Juvenile wild Chinook from throughout the Salish Sea forage in the San Juan Islands from May to September, at 65-200 mm fork lengths. To determine the resource requirements of these fish and monitor their nutritional status, we have set a 120-foot seine in 2-3 fathoms of water every other week when salmon are present in two heavily utilized bays, and gut lavaged up to 50 wild fish/day. Data for nearly 2,000 fish lavaged in 2009-2012 suggest that juvenile herring are the preferred prey but are only bioavailable when they are less than one-third of the length of the salmon. Such small herring are rarely seen in the islands, most likely because of the historical decline of herring spawning in the islands. When herring are not bioavailable, sandlance are most likely to be taken instead; sandlance are bioavailable up to 60% of the length of the salmon. Smelt comprise less than one percent of fish taken by juvenile Chinook. Crustaceans and terrestrials comprise most of the juvenile Chinook when herring or sandlance are absent or too large to handle. Juvenile Chinook and nesting seabirds near our Lopez Island and Waldron Island study sites may both compete for limited local herring stocks and default to consuming sandlance.

Studies of Eulachon Smelt in Oregon and Washington

Phillip Dionne[1], Erick Van Dyke[2], Lorna Wargo[1]

[1]*Washington Department of Fish and Wildlife,*
[2]*Oregon Department of Fish and Wildlife*

Since 2010 Washington Department of Fish and Wildlife (WDFW) and Oregon Department of Fish and Wildlife (ODFW) have collaborated on a three year project to monitor eulachon (*Thaleichthys pacificus*) by-catch in pink shrimp (*Pandalus borealis*) fisheries, and better document the abundance and distribution of eulachon in the Columbia River and document their spawning in Oregon and Washington rivers. Preliminary results from the first two years of this project to determine presence/absence of spawning found potential eulachon larvae in five of 16 rivers sampled outside of the Columbia basin. Larvae sampling in the Columbia River demonstrated a likely spawning window from November through May, and preliminary larval abundance estimates from the winter/spring of 2011 indicate that approximately 590 billion eulachon eggs were spawned in the Columbia River and its tributaries. Now entering the third and final year of the study, efforts to monitor larvae density in the Columbia River will continue, but will be partnered with efforts by the NOAA Pt. Adams Research Station to collect pre-spawn adult eulachon in the lower estuary to assess sex ratio and fecundity.

Did an Oil Spill Contribute to the Decline of Cherry Point Herring?

Fred Felleman, WAVE Consulting

Maintaining abundant and diverse forage fish is crucial to the recovery of many avian and marine species of the Salish Sea. The Puget Sound Leadership Council included Pacific herring as one of 21 "Dash Board Indicators" of its recovery in U.S. waters. However, the actions needed to achieve those goals remain to be defined.

The genetically distinct Cherry Point herring stock has declined from 15,000 tons of spawning biomass in the 1970s, to less than 800 tons currently. The purported migratory nature of this stock has been used to assert that anthropogenic impacts from the construction and operation of three industrial facilities, and associated docks, ships and wastewater discharges along the spawning beds have had negligible impact on the stock. Uncertainty surrounding the cause of this decline has not resulted in research or recovery efforts despite the proposed construction of the Gateway Coal terminal.

New information is presented on a major oil spill that occurred during a record high herring spawn (Bellingham Herald 6/8/72) the year prior to the stock's decline. The chronic acoustic, visual and water quality impacts associated with the existing industrial facilities are also suggested to be contributors to the stock' failure to recover.

Intensive studies following the *Exxon Valdez* and *Cosco Busan* oil spills document the significant impacts of PAH exposure during early life stages. Spinal deformities are increasingly prevalent from Cherry Point downstream of the NPDES discharges. These impacts are exacerbated by UV light, to which spring spawning stocks such as Cherry Point are particularly exposed.

Evidence for the Portfolio Effect in Pacific Herring in Puget Sound, Washington

Tessa B. Francis, University of Washington/ Puget Sound Institute

Effective management of Puget Sound forage fish requires an understanding of the natural and human drivers behind year-to-year fluctuations in population abundances. Current management strategies for Pacific herring in Puget Sound are based on the genetic differentiation between three separate stocks/stock complexes. However, additional characteristics may contribute to the diversity of the entire Puget Sound metapopulation. Here, we consider whether there is a portfolio effect in herring, where the entire Puget Sound herring stock is buffered against broad abundance fluctuations by the diversity of multiple populations. Using annual adult spawning biomass data collected by WDFW for each herring population (1973-2011), we found that abundance patterns varied among the populations and there was little regional coherence. For several populations, their maximum contribution to total Puget Sound herring biomass was up to 10 times their mean contribution. The variability of individual population spawning biomass was more than 3 times the variability of Puget Sound-wide biomass across the time series. We found many negative correlations between the time series of individual population biomass. Finally, we found little regional coherence, in that the abundances of populations within regions were not more coherent than populations across regions. These patterns demonstrate that population-level diversity not derived from genetic differentiation is associated with abundance patterns. These results indicate the need for conservative management strategies aimed at maintaining the resilience in Puget Sound herring, particularly in light of their key role in the marine food web.

Investigations of Early Life History of Surf Smelt and Pacific Sand Lance in Puget Sound: Some Preliminary Findings and Planned Future Activities

Theresa L. Liedtke, Dennis W. Rondorf, Collin D. Smith, and Renee Takesue
U.S. Geological Survey

Pacific sand lance (*Ammodytes hexapterus*) and surf smelt (*Hypomesus pretiosus*) use the beaches of Puget Sound for spawning and egg incubation, but little is known of the movements or distribution of these fish beyond the spawning period. Considering that nearshore habitats (such as eelgrass) are often used as nursery and rearing grounds by other fish species, we investigated the use of nearshore areas by the juvenile life stages of these fish relative to areas with bare substrates. We also investigated the influence of the shoreline configuration: we compared juvenile forage fish use of open shorelines vs. embayments. Small embayments are valuable habitats for juvenile salmon and other fish species, and may serve this role for forage fish as well. Combining these two questions we selected 11 study sites in Central Puget Sound that were either open shorelines or embayments, with eelgrass or bare substrate. Our study objectives included: (1) measure abundance of juvenile forage fish in each of the four habitat types, (2) describe the extent and characteristics of eelgrass beds at study sites, and (3) describe food habits of juvenile surf smelt and sand lance captured in eelgrass habitats. We completed 330 beach seine hauls in May and June 2012, during both day and night conditions, and captured over 2,500 surf smelt and 59,000 sand lance. The total catch was dominated by sand lance, which were captured infrequently, in very high numbers. For surf smelt, the highest percentage of fish were captured in embayments with bare substrates (38%), and the lowest percentages were captured in embayments with eelgrass (14%). For sand lance, almost all catches were in bare habitats, with less than 1% of catches in eelgrass. A slightly higher percentage of fish were captured in embayments (56%) compared to open shorelines (43%). Analyses of habitat preferences are ongoing and analyses of juvenile forage fish food habitats in eelgrass will be conducted during summer of 2013.

Quantitative Assessment of Surf Smelt and Pacific Sand Lance Spawn Deposition

Shannon Miller and Randy Hatch
Point No Point Treaty Council

Most investigations of intertidal forage fish reproduction have been qualitative, useful for documenting spatio-temporal spawning distributions. Quantitative methods for assessing trends in egg abundance are lacking, however. We began a pilot study at Indian Island Naval Magazine in October 2011, to develop a standardized sampling protocol to establish annual indices of surf smelt (*Hypomesus pretiosus*) and Pacific sand lance (*Ammodytes hexapterus*) spawning success. A stainless steel quadrate frame was used to remove 0.05 m^2 substrate samples at random points in the +5 to +10 foot tidal elevation range. Samples were later placed in an inverted 1 L plastic cone and water pumped upwards at a rate of 3 gallons per minute (i.e., elutriation). Rinsing caused heavier materials (sand, pebbles) to circulate while lighter materials (eggs, shell, silt) were forced out of the funnel into a retention sieve. Validity of the elutriation process was tested by examining 30 seeded replicates. Elutriation recovered 97 % of surf smelt eggs and 74 % of Pacific sand lance eggs. Catch-per-unit-effort (CPUE) of both species averaged 390 eggs/sample over the 6-month sample period. Smelt CPUE peaked in November (2,000 eggs/sample) and sand lance CPUE peaked in December (600 eggs/sample). Coefficient of variation among subsamples was high (>2.0) in some cases, indicating a patchy distribution of spawn. Sample design modifications are ongoing to provide more precise estimates of egg deposition.

Historic Sampling Effort and Nearshore Distribution of Pacific Sand Lance (*Ammodytes hexapterus*) in the Salish Sea, Washington

James Selleck (Wahsington Departmen of Fish and Wildlife), Caroline Gibson (Northwest Straits Commission), Suzanne Shull (Washington State Department of Ecology/ Padilla Bay NERR, and Joseph Gaydos (SeaDoc Society)

Pacific sand lance are an important food web component in the Salish Sea. These energy-dense fish constitute important prey for a variety of salmonids, groundfish, marine mammals, and seabirds. Sand lance have been well documented in nearshore surveys in Puget Sound since the 1970s, yet little life history or biological information is available outside of intertidal spawning habitat use. We conducted a retrospective analysis of nearshore sand lance distribution using historical data to elucidate basic biological parameters. Beach seine and tow net data were gathered from federal, state and county agencies, tribes, universities, private consulting businesses, and non-profit organizations. We compiled 15,192 records collected between 1970 and 2009, from 1431 unique sites, representing 13% of Puget Sound's shoreline. Sand lance were captured in 21% of the records, and during every month of the year. Sites were separated into seven watershed basins. Maps were produced outlining sand lance presence and catch size by basin. Sand lance presence ranged from 58% to 95% by basin, and were present at 30% of stream mouths sampled. The maximum number of fish captured per record increased between May and August. The northern basins comprised 87% of large captures, mostly during mid-summer. A subset of the data found fork length ranging from 1.7 cm to 19.0 cm, with 6.5% of measured fish greater than 12 cm. Extensive nearshore fish surveys of Puget Sound over the past 40 years demonstrate sand lance are ubiquitous throughout the region year round, and in some instances in great abundance.

Spatial and Temporal Structure of Marine Predator-Prey Interactions in the Columbia River Plume

J.E.Zamon; E.M. Phillips; L.H. Reinalda
NOAA/ Pt. Adams Research Station

During 2003-2009, May and June oceanographic surveys on the Oregon and Washington coasts (USA) revealed anomalously high concentrations of fish-eating birds near the mouth of the Columbia River. Further ship- and land-based investigation demonstrated associations between bird predators and the tidally-driven convergence fronts separating low-salinity (12-21), recent river discharge from higher-salinity (>21) coastal waters. Mixed-species predator aggregations include both surface-feeding and diving species (e.g. gulls, pelicans, alcids, shearwaters). Aggregations were evident and recurring at fine spatial and temporal scales of meters to kilometers and hours to days. Diet items from birds captured in these areas included planktivorous forage fishes such as northern anchovy (*Engraulis mordax*), smelt (Osmeridae), and herring (Clupeidae); as well as some juvenile salmon (*Oncorhynchus spp.*). Preliminary evidence from estuary hydroacoustic surveys shows fish schools primarily below the pycnocline, suggesting salinity structure has a strong effect on spatial distribution of forage fishes. We hypothesize the tidal dynamics of the Columbia River discharge create predictable aggregations of forage fishes in time and space, and fish aggregations then attract upper trophic level predators to river plume habitat. We propose the tidal dynamics of river plumes may be a general structural mechanism affecting predator-prey interactions in locations where river discharge affects coastal habitat.

Identified Priority Needs and Actions

Day 2 of the symposium was designed to foster discussions among participants in order to develop priority science and policy needs and actions for forage fish in Washington and British Columbia. Although a variety of species and geographic regions were discussed on day 1 to provide background, the goal of the group discussions on day 2 was to focus on the forage fish species present in the Salish Sea, making the resultant priority needs and actions regionally relevant.

To meet this objective in the limited time available on day 2, participants were asked to submit written ideas of suggested research and policy needs and actions during the first day. Day 1 presentations initiated hearty discussion among participants and resulted in numerous written suggestions. The written suggestions were compiled by symposium support staff, and used as a starting point for group discussions on day 2. Facilitators were pre-selected to host the science (Joseph Gaydos) and policy (Kit Rawson) working groups and participants were invited to contribute input to the group of their choice. Each working group began by projecting the summary of the written contributions from day 1. Then the group moved through the list, adding comments and merging similar comments into themes, to arrive at the consensus list. The facilitators and organizing committee made it clear to the participants that the list was intended to be a compilation of priority needs and actions, but the items would not be ranked. All listed needs and actions held equal priority on the broad scale and the compiled lists spanned a variety of focal research and management topics.

Following the individual working groups, all participants reconvened to hear summaries generated by the working groups. This session was designed to allow science group members to provide input into the policy list, and vice versa. Joseph Gaydos and Kit Rawson presented the summaries for their respective working groups and comments were incorporated into the lists.

Immediately following the symposium, the draft lists of science and policy needs and actions were circulated to all symposium participants for review. Comments and clarifications specific to information provided at the symposium were submitted to the organizing committee, and incorporated into the summaries presented below.

Priority Science Needs

The Science Work Group generated a list of five priority needs to support the conservation and precautionary management of forage fish in the Salish Sea. These were categories for which work group participants stated that information was lacking, posing challenges for effective management.

- **Natural History Information**

    The group discussed the overall lack of information on the natural history of forage fish in the Salish Sea. The life history of some species is better known than for others, for example we know more about herring than we do about sand lance, but additional natural history information for all species would be useful to inform managers and guide industrial (i.e., dredging) and restoration activities. The data gaps include a thorough understanding of stock structure, spatiotemporal distribution, behavior, and habitat requirements throughout all life stages. Participants suggested a synthesis of existing data, especially from field studies, an effort to generate natural history narratives for each species, and the construction of temporal conceptual models (including anecdotal information) as actions that could be taken to begin to meet this need.

A discussion on genetic stock delineation highlighted some recent findings and specific needs. A study of surf smelt genetics (WDFW and USGS) suggests there is a single stock of surf smelt in Puget Sound, but some additional analyses are needed to examine outlier stocks. Some anecdotal information suggests differences in sand lance life histories that might be influenced by stock structure, so the group put forward the need to assess sand lance genetics.

- **Habitat Protection and Habitat Quality Information**

There are significant knowledge gaps related to forage fish habitat requirements. Managers cannot effectively protect or restore habitats critical for forage fish if species requirements are not known at all life stages. The group defined specific applications for habitat protection information, including informing Hydraulic Project Approval (HPA, managed by WDFW) and Section 404 (U.S. Army Corps of Engineers) permitting decisions. Shoreline spawning species of forage fish are vulnerable to habitat degradation due to human activity impacts on the shoreline. One specific need that came from group discussion was definitive information on the impacts of shoreline armoring on forage fish that spawn in the intertidal zone. Additional information needs included a better understanding of the temporal consistency of beach use by intertidal spawners (i.e., surf smelt and sand lance), the use of deep-water sandforms by sand lance, an effort to quantify the importance of specific habitat types, and the effects of habitat quality (such as toxic exposure and shading) on the early life history and recruitment of all forage fish species.

- **Trophic Interaction Information**

More information is needed on the role of forage fish in the marine food web, including the diet needs of forage fish and their predators. The group was specifically interested in comprehensive food web modeling (expanding current models and using new models) using the entire Salish Sea (versus modeling subbasins) to best account for heterogeneity in the system. Inputs to these models include knowledge about species abundance and distribution, as well as consumption and metabolic efficiency data, which ties this need to other needs identified by the group. Ultimately, this approach should help to define the specific role of each forage fish species in the ecosystem and to quantify the forage fish biomass that is needed to support local predator species. Predators will consume forage fish regardless of any established fisheries quotas that are set, so managers need to define a predator reserve or predator buffer and build it into harvest control rules in order to maintain the health of the ecosystem. Input that would be useful to support this effort includes local, long-term datasets on the use of forage fish by predators, conducting isotope analysis of existing samples, evaluations of the food base for forage fish (plankton abundance), and modeling the potential impacts of forage fish bycatch in trawl fisheries in Washington and British Columbia. Using online data sharing was proposed as a procedure that could be developed or expanded to support these information needs.

- **Consideration of All Stressors**

     The group recommended efforts to identify abundance-limiting stress or mortality factors throughout forage fish life histories. Although much of the historical information on forage fish in the Salish Sea is based in the nearshore environment, it is important to note that the majority of forage fish life histories are in the pelagic realm. Consideration of stressors should include both the nearshore and the pelagic environments, all life stages (eggs through spawning adults), and both lethal and sub-lethal effects, with a linkage to impacts at the population level. Examples of stressors discussed by the group include pathogens, toxic contaminants (including endocrine disruptors), changing climate conditions, disturbance or loss of critical habitat, and commercial and recreational fisheries. Further effort is needed to identify potential stressors and evaluate their impacts. For example, what is the impact on fish that are intercepted but not landed in shrimp trawl fisheries? Canada's Department of Fisheries and Oceans is working to develop a bycatch and discard policy to address some of these stressors. Linkages between stressors also need to be investigated, for example the potential interactions between contaminants and infectious disease in forage fish.

     Several species-specific research actions were identified by the group. One action was a multi-stage, iterative approach to mitigating disease impacts to forage fish populations, including surveys to detect disease and the development of tools to predict disease potential. Other identified actions include evaluation of nearshore toxics on larval development and spawning activity, using a paired study design to investigate anthropogenic factors influencing sand lance recruitment and distribution, and investigating the cause of decline in Cherry Point herring to guide recovery efforts.

- **Monitoring**

     Monitoring needs discussed by the working group were diverse and provided support to the other identified priority science needs. The lack of a reliable, and stock-specific, abundance estimate is a large data gap for most forage fish species in the Salish Sea. It is difficult to assess whether forage fish populations are stable, growing, or declining without a baseline population estimate and a means of assessing abundance on a relevant time scale. Herring are the only forage fish species in Puget Sound that are regularly monitored (by WDFW), and the group recommended that future effort be more balanced across all forage fish species. To achieve this goal, an evaluation of monitoring mechanisms and indices of abundance is needed (e.g., net vs. acoustic surveys), with consideration to approaches that use egg and larval surveys. Additional effort also is recommended in fishery monitoring, especially non-commercial catch, in all of its forms, including recreational, tribal, and bycatch. Data are lacking on the timing and location of forage fish spawning and migration on the coasts of Washington and British Columbia, although a new effort to survey the Washington coastline was initiated by WDFW and tribal co-managers in September 2012. To enhance oil spill preparedness, the group recommends baseline surveys of polycyclic aromatic hydrocarbons (PAHs) in known critical habitats, such as spawning beaches and eelgrass beds. Finally, the group noted that a systematic monitoring effort would improve our understanding of the regional marine ecology. All suggested monitoring efforts would benefit from improved coordination among State and Federal agencies and Tribes as well as non-profit entities, industry, and volunteer organizations (e.g., Marine Resource Committees).

Priority Policy Needs

The Policy Work Group generated a list of eight priority needs to support the conservation and precautionary management of forage fish in the Salish Sea. These were categories for which work group participants recommended actions that could prove effective in improving management goals and outcomes.

- **Address All Threats During Restoration Planning and Implementation**

    This action emphasizes the need to base management strategies on, and implement existing policies for, the concurrent evaluation of all threats to forage fish. Specifically it calls for management through the "ecosystem lens" when plans are developed for protection and restoration of forage fish, incorporating threats such as habitat loss or degradation, climate change, and fishing pressure. Currently (2012), at least in Washington, there are significant gaps in how forage fish are managed because the harvest formula proposed in the 1998 Forage Fish Management Plan requires valid estimates of population abundance and harvest, both of which are lacking for most species. Additionally, the capacity for in-season management of these resources is lacking due to staffing and funding shortfalls. The working group recommended several actions, including taking a conservative approach to setting harvest guidelines and permitting of new fisheries and new gear types, using appropriately-sized marine protected areas to ensure protection of forage fish throughout their life cycle, cleaning up polychlorinated biphenyls (PCBs), and reducing the use of fossil fuels in an effort to reduce PAHs. In Canada, there are several policies in place that address multiple threats to forage fish, but further progress is needed toward implementing them for all fisheries.

- **Revise Management Framework to Address Ecosystem Role of Forage Fish Niche**

    It is widely recognized that forage fish abundance in a localized region can fluctuate broadly over a series of years in response to a combination of factors, including ocean conditions, recruitment success, predation pressure, fishery intensity, and habitat quantity and quality. As species often respond differently to these factors, it is important to consider the ecosystem role of the forage base in aggregate, rather than on a species-specific basis. The working group recognized that managing the abundance of, fishery pressure on, and protection of habitat for the multispecies "forage fish niche" requires information on population and food web dynamics that may not yet be available. However, the science working group recommended a focus on research on trophic interactions that could be applied to this management need.

- **Craft Messages To Create And Enhance Public Awareness**

    Public awareness of forage fish, what they are and their important role in the ecosystem, is lacking and should be improved to support forage fish management. Because the definition of 'forage fish' can be variable, one priority action would be to develop and distribute a clear definition of forage fish to the general public (especially in Washington and British Columbia). One approach might be to use compelling natural history narratives of the forage fish, linking them to the more charismatic species they support, such as salmon, orcas, and seabirds. Several small working groups could each prepare short narratives and combine them with some color images to create information pamphlets for distribution. The goal of this public awareness campaign would be a public that is supportive of forage fish conservation measures because they acknowledge the importance of these fish species.

- **Develop and Enforce Fisheries Rules That Support Sustainable Management**

    More explicit mechanisms are needed to aid the integration of science into policy and management decisions. In cases where the need to use science to guide management is expressed, the actual mechanisms by which to execute this goal are not clear or consistently applied. One specific action identified by the working group applies to Washington, where they recommend licensing recreational harvest of surf smelt in Puget Sound (commercial harvest is currently licensed). A related need in Canada is for monitoring of both the commercial and recreational catches of surf smelt (see Priority Science Needs, Monitoring).

- **Identify Opportunities To Protect Forage Fish Through Existing Mechanisms**

    A comprehensive review of existing mechanisms that could enhance protection of forage fish needs to be undertaken. For example, protection opportunities may exist using the critical habitat designation of the Endangered Species Act (ESA), or the designation of essential fish habitat under the Magnuson-Stevens Act (MSA). Under the MSA the Pacific Fisheries Management Council (and other regional fisheries councils) can designate forage fish as "essential fish habitat" for other species (16 U.S.C. 1853(a)(7); MSA 303 (a)(7)). Another mechanism might be the consideration of prey items for fish protected under the ESA in Section 7 Consultation documents. For example, the U.S. Army Corps of Engineers conducts dredging that entrains sand lance, but no constraints are used to guide the dredging since sand lance have no ESA protection. If links are made to ESA-listed species that consume sand lance (e.g., salmon), then restrictions could be put in place to avoid or minimize disturbance to sand lance.

- **Align Washington State's 'No Net Loss' Policy With Permitting Authority Under Law**

    Washington State Administration Code defines known forage fish (herring, surf smelt, and sand lance) spawning habitat as Saltwater Habitats of Special Concern (WAC 220-110-250) and establishes a "no net loss" provision for the protection of these areas from shoreline development, including armoring. Exceptions to this provision are allowed, however, in the case of single-family residences and under certain commercial situations. Additionally, the system by which development permits are issued varies regionally and rarely involves post-construction monitoring to evaluate long-term ecological effects of the construction. Numerous unauthorized shoreline structures have been noted in Puget Sound, and permitted structures may not be built to specifications for a variety of reasons. This priority need requires close coordination between the management authorities within WDFW's habitat and enforcement divisions and revisions to policies and initiatives governing shoreline development, including the Habitat Conservation Plan (HCP) and Critical Area Ordinances.

- **Develop Specific Language on Forage Fish Under Existing WA-BC Cooperative Agreements**

    Forage fish protection efforts could be aided by inserting specific language on their role and requirements into existing transboundary agreements. Specific agreements discussed by the working group include the Pacific Coast Collaborative, the West Coast Governor's Alliance, the Pacific Salmon Commission, and the National Ocean Council.

- **Establish a Transboundary Forage Fish Task Force and Working Group**

    The group recommended establishing a transboundary forage fish task force and a working group. One example for the task force, although not exactly the model suggested, is the International Pacific Halibut and Salmon Commissions. A Forage Fish Working Group should be established and affiliated with the Puget Sound Partnership. The task force could conduct a comprehensive assessment of historical and current forage fish science and management, incorporating the findings of Governor Gregoire's Blue Ribbon Panel on Ocean Acidification (Fall 2012). The task force could then develop specific ecosystem-based objectives for forage fish management that recognize the key role of forage fish in the complex marine food web. Finally, the task force could develop a plan for implementing the priority policy needs and actions identified here to achieve these management objectives. The Forage Fish Working Group could then actively pursue implementation of these recommendations through the auspices of the Puget Sound Partnership. There was wide support for this policy action, among both the policy and the science working groups. The trans-boundary biennial research conference, the Salish Sea Ecosystem Conference, provides a constructive venue for scientist and managers to consider such a strategy for cooperation across the international border. Sustained long-term funding for the task force was identified as a need.

Appendix A. Participant List

PARTICIPANT LIST

2012 Friday Harbor Laboratories Symposium
Conservation and Ecology of Marine Forage Fishes
September 12-14, 2012

Last Name	First Name	Affiliation	Email
Barsh	Russel	KWIAHT	RLBarsh@gmail.com
Beamer	Eric	Skagit River System Cooperative	ebeamer@skagitcoop.org
Boldt	Jennifer	Fisheries and Oceans Canada	Jennifer.Boldt@dfo-mpo.gc.ca
Chapman	Alan	Lummi Nation	alanc@lummi-nsn.gov
Cheng	Henry	WA Dept. of Fish and Wildlife	Yuk.cheng@dfw.wa.gov
Davis *	Shannon	FRIENDS of the San Juans	shannon@sanjuans.org
Dionne	Phillip	WA Dept. of Fish and Wildlife	Phillip.dionne@dfw.wa.gov
Donnelly	Robert	US Army Corps of Engineers	Robert.F.Donnelly@usace.army mil
Dublanica	Keith	Recreation and Conservation Office	keith.dublanica@rco.wa.gov
Dye	Paul	The Nature Conservancy	pdye@tnc.org
Dzinbal	Ken	Puget Sound Partnership	ken.dzinbal@psp.wa.gov
English	Collin	Freelance consultant - communication	collin.english@gmail.com
Essington	Tim	University of Washington	essing@u.washington.edu
Fagergren	Duane	Puget Sound Partnership	duane.fagergren@psp.wa.gov
Felleman	Fred	WAVE Consulting	felleman@comcast.net
Francis	Tessa	UW/ Puget Sound Institute	tessa@uw.edu
Fredrickson	Ivy	Ocean Conservancy	ifredrickson@oceanconservancy.org
Gaydos	Joseph	SeaDoc Society	jkgaydos@ucdavis.edu
Gibson*	Caroline	Northwest Straits Commission	gibson@nwstraits.org
Gleason	Nancy	US Army Corps of Engineers	nancy.c.gleason@usace.army mil
Hay	Doug	Nearshore Research	hay.doug@shaw.ca
Hershberger	Paul	U.S. Geological Survey	phershberger@usgs.gov
Hood*	Andrea	Northwest Straits Commission	hood@nwstraits.org
Hunt	George	University of Washington	geohunt2@uw.edu
Hurtado	Felipe	University of Washington	fhurtado@u.washington.edu
Kaplan	Isaac	NOAA/ NW Fisheries Science Center	isaac kaplan@noaa.gov
Koch	Kyle	Skagit Fisheries Enhancement Group	kyle@skagitfisheries.org
Krueger	Kirk	WA Dept. of Fish and Wildlife	Kirk.Krueger@dfw.wa.gov
Liedtke	Theresa	U.S. Geological Survey	tliedtke@usgs.gov
Lindquist	Adam	WA Dept. of Fish and Wildlife	Adam.Lindquist@dfw.wa.gov
Lloyd	David	San Juan Marine Resources Committee	lloyd@islandtransit.org
Lowry	Dayv	WA Dept. of Fish and Wildlife	Dayv.Lowry@dfw.wa.gov
Marx	Steve	Pew Environment Group	smarx@pewtrusts.org
Miller	Shannon	Point No Point Treaty Council	smiller@pnptc.org
Moran	Patrick	U.S. Geological Survey	pwmoran@usgs.gov
Ormseth	Olav	NOAA/ Alaska Fisheries Science Center	olav.ormseth@noaa.gov
Pearson	Scott	WA Dept. of Fish and Wildlife	Scott.Pearson@dfw.wa.gov
Penttila	Dan	Salish Sea Biological	depenttila@fidalgo.net
Pokorny	Tami	Jefferson Co. Water Resources	tpokorny@co.jefferson.wa.us
Rabourn	Greg	King Co. Dept. of Natural Res. & Parks	greg rabourn@kingcounty.gov
Rawson	Kit	Tulalip Tribes	krawson@tulaliptribes-nsn.gov

Rice	Casey	NOAA/ NW Fisheries Science Center	casimir rice@noaa.gov
Robinson	Erik	Pew Environment Group	erobinson@pewtrusts.org
Runnells	Emily	University of Washington	esrunnells@gmail.com
Schlenger	Paul	Confluence Environmental Company	paul.schlenger@confenv.com
Selleck	James	WA Dept. of Fish and Wildlife	James.selleck@earthlink net
Small	Doris	WA Dept. of Fish and Wildlife	doris.small@dfw.wa.gov
Stedman	Bruce	Stedman & Associates	brucestedman1@gmail.com
Stick	Kurt	WA Dept. of Fish and Wildlife	stickkcs@dfw.wa.gov
Stockwell	Jason	University of Vermont	jdstockw@uvm.edu
Summers	Adam	University of Washington/ Friday Harbor Labs	fishguy@u.washington.edu
Thayer	Julie	Farallon Institute for Adv Ecosystem Research	jthayer@faralloninstitute.org
Van Cleve*	Brie	FB Van Cleve & Associates	brie.van.cleve@gmail.com
Waldbillig	Chris	WA Dept. of Fish and Wildlife	Chris.Waldbillig@dfw.wa.gov
Wargo	Lorna	WA Dept. of Fish and Wildlife	lorna.wargo@dfw.wa.gov
West	Jim	WA Dept. of Fish and Wildlife	james.west@dfw.wa.gov
Whitman	Tina	FRIENDS of the San Juans	tina@sanjuans.org
Zamon	Jeanette	NOAA/ Pt. Adams Research Station	jen.zamon@noaa.gov

*Staff support